M000017113

NO ORDINARY LIZ

An extraordinary
story of life & family

To: Peggy
Always Choose to be
Extraordinary

Elizabeth Sutherland

NOW
PUBLISHING

1.888.5069-NOW
www.nowscpress.com
@nowscpress

Ordering Information:
Quantity sales. Special discounts are available on quantity purchases by corporations, associations, and others. For details, contact the publisher at the address above.

Orders by U.S. trade bookstores and wholesalers. Please contact: NOW SC Press: Tel: (888) 5069-NOW or visit www.nowscpress.com.

Printed in the United States of America
First Printing, 2018
ISBN: 978-0-9995845-8-3

About the Cover: Why butterflies? Butterflies represent the beauty of change, finding a new life, being agile and adaptable and in the process, releasing good into the world. Every butterfly is unique, and until it emerges from the cocoon, no one knows what the butterfly will look like. It's the same with each one of us—we are butterflies in the making, and our lives can go from ugly to beautiful. We are all individuals, and we are all awe-inspiring. So be a butterfly--accept who you are as an individual and allow yourself the opportunity to fly and be free.

** All names in this story have been changed to protect identities, unless otherwise noted.

Dedication

Dedicated To
God:
For protecting me through all the hard years
when I couldn't protect myself

My past:
For guiding me down the road less traveled

My future:
For allowing me to walk in my purpose

My brother, Jonathan and my sister, Melissa:
The greatest gift life ever gave me is you

Evelyn & Gene:
For giving me a second chance to live the life I
deserve

Rhondi, Jif, Janna and Shanna:
For being there when Melissa and I really needed
you, for genuinely opening your home and your
hearts to us, and for being the loving family we
never had. You have changed our lives forever in
the most beautiful way and we are beyond blessed
to call you our family. We are eternally grateful for
the love and support you have always given us.

My nieces and nephews:
Teagan Marie, Mallory, Hagan, Madox, Cooper,
Hannah and Harley
For bringing me so much joy being their Aunt
Wiz.

My friends:
For becoming my chosen family

Foster youth of all ages:
This story is for you

Foster Parents:
For rewriting a child's story

People who give their time

Foreword

Have you ever met someone for the first time and instantly felt a connection? Whether it was a co-worker, a friend, or a spouse, there was something that immediately drew you to that person. That was the case for Elizabeth (Liz) Sutherland and myself that summer day when we met for lunch at a local sandwich shop. She came with a co-worker of mine, and the more we talked, the more we learned that we shared parallel paths. Liz grew up living in the foster care system; I worked in the foster care system for the past twenty-five years, while she was growing up and making her way through foster care homes. She was currently a Guardian ad Litem volunteer; I had just left that agency after serving in the same capacity for eleven years. The young man she was an advocate for attended my Toast Masters meeting a week earlier and was a foster child in need of basic-need items. I had met the young man without knowing the connection and I am currently the director of a program that provides such items for foster children. Her employer was searching for a place to do volunteer work in the community and my program offered a location for corporate in-service days. The more she shared her life story and her vision for helping foster kids with me, the more we connected. I quickly recognized that her story is the reason I get up and to work every day…to make a difference for foster children. We were meant to meet. Fate brought us together and our connection sealed our bond.

Foster care is a world most of the public would choose not to see; it is just too hard to imagine and is painful for most of us to feel. How could someone hurt a child? Please know that no child asks to come to foster care. They are brought into foster care— sadly through no fault of their own—as victims of child abuse, neglect, and/or abandonment. For their safety, they are removed from the only home they know. They go to live with kind strangers; sometimes with little belongings from home and sometimes with their belongings shoved into a trash bag. Liz was one of these children.

The day DCFS showed up at her North Carolina home, thirteen-year-old Liz was elated. Someone was coming to save her from a home filled with physical and emotional abuse. Somebody did care! She was safe now! As the caseworker's car pulled away, she sat in the back seat and watched her home fade from view. Nervously, she clutched an orange trash bag with what she had left inside it.

Unbeknownst to Liz, the reality of foster care was about to rip off her rose-colored glasses and stomp them into dust. Separated from her two siblings and no family to reunify with, she was alone in foster care—except for that orange trash bag. A trash bag is meant to hold trash, not a child's life treasures. That bag soon became her identity as she moved from foster home to foster home. New homes, new smells, new rules, new schools, new friends…over and over. Every time she got comfortable and felt she could relax it was time to move again.

At eighteen, Liz aged out of foster care and was left to fend for herself. Independence was a scary place but she had dreams. She dreamed of an education, of finding her brother and sister, and of traveling. There were obstacles in her path, but the dreams remained.

Liz's story will take you into the world of foster care from the child's point of view. You will follow her on her journey, feel what she felt, see what she saw. Help came from unlikely sources. She survived. Her book will show you how positive influences and resiliency took her from a dark world to one filled with light and love.

Miliere said, "The greater the obstacle, the more glory in overcoming it." Determined to not be a foster care statistic, Liz worked hard to overcome her life's circumstances. It certainly was not an easy journey, but it was her journey to become the woman she is today. She owns her background and her story. She knows it does not define her and is brave enough to share it to inspire and motivate others. It is now her calling. Liz has shared her story with me. Now she is sharing it with you. I hope you also feel connected and motivated to make a difference!

Kelly Rossi
Director, Eckerd Connects Raising Hope
Clearwater, FL

An Open Letter to Other Foster Kids

This is where your story begins. Your life was just interrupted. You've been taken away from your parents, siblings, the comfort of your own bed, and the life you grew to know. I know you're in shock. I was. You've just entered your first foster home or group home. Alone. Not all foster placements will be the same. Some homes may have two children while others may have ten. Some foster parents may show some sort of affection, while others not so much. That is okay, though. It's all part of the journey.

Your entire life is in a bag and your foundation is broken; all your trust, loyalty and any faith you had in humanity is lost. You feel abandoned by everyone.

I know you're scared, shocked, and frightened right now. That you're just trying to process what happened. Right now, all you want to do is go back to where you were, regardless of any physical abuse or neglect. You want one more opportunity to hug your sister or brother. Maybe you're depressed and want to cry. Maybe you're angry and want to hit something. You have every right to feel all of this. Your life is changing and you're about to embark on a wild ride.

You will experience pain. Lots of it. You will find happiness and joy where you least expect it. You will long for stability, to be loved, cared for, and protected. Right now, you have no safety net. You are owned by the state. Just breathe. You're okay! Grieve, cry, laugh, feel your emotions, but whatever you do, *please* don't blame yourself. This is not your fault, not in any way.

Don't succumb to the numbness of drugs and alcohol. They are temporary patches for emotions you need to feel. Be strong. Be courageous. After all, you are a survivor. Don't be afraid to ask for help and don't be afraid to lean on others when you feel weak.

Foster kids have a weapon in life that most don't. Resilience. We are strong, and we always bounce back from whatever is thrown our way. Don't let people put a label on you. Instead, label yourself as strong, courageous and proud. In the back of this book, there are resources and tips to help you navigate the future.

Focus on what makes you happy. You may be saying, "I don't know what does." That's okay. If you like to sing, sing. If you like music, write music.

If your passion is writing, write stories. Find your outlet.

Your story doesn't end here. It's the beginning—and the chapters ahead are up to you. Be proud of who you are. And always remember: You are worth it. You are amazing. You are loved.

Someday, your story will give others hope, purpose, and a sense of belonging. Start living that story right now.

I will always love you,
Former Foster Youth

Table of Contents

Chapter 1

Sundays

*T*here is something mesmerizing about opening up an old church hymnal, flipping to your favorite songs, and singing them as loud as your soul can stand. The rustic smell of a white little country church, the rise and fall of other voices joining in— in that moment you've created a family built on worship.

Family was the one thing I wanted all my life, but it was the one thing I didn't have. Instead, I spent my childhood raised by strangers, abused and forgotten, displaced and abandoned. At the age of five, a man I don't remember dropped me and my siblings off at his mother's house, told us she was our grandmother, and that we were living here from now on. He dropped us off so fast, he left nothing behind but a cloud of gravel dust.

Other kids' first memories are of riding a bike or finding a present from Santa on Christmas morning. My first memory is this—being left with a woman who didn't want us. I've been told my own mother paid an elderly lady in Rota, Spain to care for us three. When our mother didn't send over the payment for us, the woman threatened to turn us out on the streets. I always wondered what kind of trouble my mother was in for her to give up on us so easily. What was her living situation like? Why couldn't another family member take us in? Was she living out on the streets and was trying to do the best she could? Did her family not want her if she brought home three children? Most of all, I have one burning question that's never been answered . . . *why*?

That moment my mother got behind on her payments, a man neatly dressed in a Navy uniform intervened and took us from Spain to Waynesville, North Carolina. I don't know why he did that or what his intentions were. All I knew was that we escaped one possible hell for another one far worse. I don't remember any of that time in Spain. Maybe it's because I have no information that I have mixed emotions about that part of my history and so many questions in my head: Were we abused? Were we fed enough? Where did we sleep? Were the three of us always kept together? Perhaps something so traumatic occurred that my mind decided to block it out, leaving me with the urge to know more.

I do, however, remember our life in North Carolina. We lived in a rusty yellow trailer on a hill that was surrounded by dozens of others, like a line of pencils in a box. The trailers were all different colors, shapes, and sizes. Some had added man-made garages fashioned out of wood scraps and tin roofs, with nothing holding them down but some old rubber tires. Some had oversized porches and cement blocks as stairs. The neighborhood and the trailer were crowded with three kids and our "grandmother", but the lot had a big wooded area in the back and a big open area in the front that was later converted into a park. The park was pretty big. It looked like half of a football field and was surrounded by big and small trees and scattered dirt patches. The second we were free to have a moment to ourselves, my brother, sister and I would run out the door of the single-wide to play with the other children in the trailer park. Sometimes we'd go with permission, sometimes we'd sneak out.

I remember being on that playground and feeling envious as I watched families play with their kids. Their parents would toss them a red rubber kickball, push them on the tire swing, or give them a hand as they tried to climb a tree. All

> I remember being on that playground and feeling envious as I watched families play with their kids.

the while, the kids laughed and smiled. The hardest part was watching them walk away and seeing their parents wrapping their arms around them in a hug. Even dysfunctional families seemed normal to me because I lacked a family of my own.

The woman who was supposedly our grandmother, a short wiry woman with a temper larger than the state of Texas, would stand on the porch and yell for us. We could hear the echo of Martha's voice through the park. And in those moments we would freeze—we knew what was coming once we climbed back up that hill.

There wasn't a day that went by that didn't consist of the back of her hand, the side of a belt buckle, or the stings of a hickory stick hitting us. We were her punching bag, her outlet for frustration. Frustration caused by her son who had dropped us off with no warning. Frustration caused by living in poverty and having so many mouths to feed. Frustrated with the world that had wronged her.

There was so much hatred bundled up in one person. The amount of physical and mental abuse could've certainly done me in and it almost did. I would lie awake in my bed at night and wonder if other kids were hearing bedtime stories, being tucked in bed, and getting hugs and kisses. I kept asking myself, "What grandmother does this to her grandchildren?"

I felt smothered, like I was a prisoner in my own life and suffocating in my reality. We lived in a three-bedroom, one-bath home. Each wall had its own story to tell. Some walls were solid dark wood and others had wild wallpaper. Mounted on the living room wall was a big deer's head with baseball caps dangling from the antlers. There were dozens of pictures in the living room but we weren't in any of them. It was mostly images of her family. We didn't have cable. Instead, we had a television with a big box on top that had aluminum foil wrapped around the arms, making it look like a gigantic spider. An oversized chest of drawers in the living room was filled with clothes that peeked out of the drawers—but not a single shirt or sweater belonged to us. The tiny house was consistently cluttered with more people and things, and never enough space. Martha's father moved in as well as her handicapped son, her daughter, and her three children. A hospital bed then overtook the living room. My siblings and I shared one full-size bed. Our dressers were made up of big boxes from the grocery store next door. Our limited supply of clothes was often a mat for the dog. He peed on them, laid on them, and got them dirty.

The TV was always on in Martha's bedroom, which was off limits. She also kept a padlock on the refrigerator. I remember being so hungry that other kids I knew in the neighborhood would sometimes sneak me snacks. If we weren't home and in bed by 5:30 p.m. each day, we were locked out of the house.

We were "rewarded" with a bath every Sunday, but were forced to use the same water when Martha was done with hers. Laundry was done once a week. The clothes on our backs were worn several days in a row regardless of how they looked or smelled. It was pretty hard to go to school with dirty, urine-stained clothes.

School was supposed to be a place to go for learning, being around like-minded people, and building new friendships. I thought it would be an escape from my reality at home, but my school life was just as harsh. School was where I found out what bullying was like. The only friends I really had growing up were my siblings and those kids in the trailer park—they were home to me.

I kept asking God why? What did I ever do to deserve this?

There was one bright spot in the horrible, dark years we lived in that trailer—Martha's father. He was a fragile old man, but also the kindest soul I ever met. He always had stains from snuff hiding in the crevices of his laugh lines, big shiny glasses that rested right above his nose, and a neatly shaved face.

One day, when Martha was beating us for some small infraction, I heard his voice behind me.

"Don't you think that's enough?" he said. He was my saving grace that day, as well as so many other days. Sometimes I would take evening walks with him. He was a man of few words, but just being able to walk alongside him was enough for me.

Growing up, it was always hard trying to figure out what to call people. I would cringe at the thought of calling someone Mom or Dad, Grandmother or Grandpa, because no one ever really acted like a parent. This one man did, in his own way. Even though he was in my life for a very short time, he left an imprint forever on my heart.

And then there were Sundays. I held on for that day because it was the only day I found a moment of peace. I can still remember how excited I was to put on my favorite little red bunny-patterned dress with the white collar. Every time I wore that dress, I felt special. I'd brush my hair, slip on a pair of scuffed white sandals and head off to church.

My sister and I would sit cross-legged in front of the big kitchen window, waiting for a car to come speeding up that gravel hill. Sometimes we had a ride to church and sometimes I'd take off with my little red bible in hand and hike up the big hill on my own. Nothing was going to stand in the way between my reality and my time with the man on the cross.

There are no words to express how I loved everything about Sundays. I loved it all—Sunday school, Bible study, singing in the choir, eating lunch with the church family, and catching a glimpse of Martha's father, who always sat in the same spot on the front right corner pew in his faded baby blue overalls.

The people in that church were so humble and didn't care about my clothes or hair or where I came from. During the holidays, I signed up to be in every church play because it meant more time spent with my church family and more time away from my reality. Since I wasn't able to eat snacks and candies back home, I looked forward to those little brown paper bags they gave out at the end. They were filled with oranges, apples, walnuts, and candy. I felt like I had hit the jackpot every time I got one! I couldn't wait to sit down on those shiny cold pews and listen to the preacher. I'd watch him praise God until he was red in the face. The passion he showed felt so good on my soul. While everything around me felt off, those moments in church felt right. This was where I needed to be.

I was always sad when it was time to leave because I never wanted it to end. Who could blame me? I wasn't ready to face the reality waiting for me at home.

Faith. I wasn't sure what it was back then, but I sincerely believe it was what got me through those years of pain and suffering while trying to find my place in the world.

Chapter 2
Blackberries

Blackberries.

If there's a scent or sight that brings me right back to my childhood, it's blackberries. For other people, their childhood memories are brought to life by the scent of fresh-cut grass, the steamy fragrance from the dryer vent, the tang of gasoline, or maybe the sound of an old song.

Even as an adult, every time I see blackberries in a grocery store or catch a glimpse of them hanging from the prickly arms of a shrub, I'm yanked back to those days.

For me, the memories are rarely good. Blackberries come part and parcel with the worst days of my life as well as the moment I escaped.

School was one of my only reprieves. I didn't complain about getting up at the break of dawn to go to school. I loved walking down that gravel road every morning, seeing the other kids from the trailer park and then climbing inside the big yellow bus.

Ours was the first stop. I scrambled to be the first one on so I could pick the seat right behind the bus driver. There were many reasons why I loved that worn brown leather seat with the stuffing peeking out of a small hole in the back. I loved watching every kid get on the bus, their cool backpacks hugged tightly to their backs. I loved pressing the side of my face against the cold window and I loved listening to the snippets of conversations floating in the air around me. The bus ride was always too short. I wanted more time—time to breathe, time to feel like an ordinary kid.

I loved school as much as I loved those early morning bus rides. I can still feel the vibrations from the bells ringing and the slamming of metal locker doors in between class periods. I was envious of all those students with their pencil cases, and backpacks, and neat, tidy book covers. Even though I had clothes on my back, I never really felt I dressed the part. The part where I was supposed to be a student in a classroom, ready to learn, fully supplied, and already fed.

Then the weekends would come. No school to break up my day and no bus ride to take me away from Martha's, except for the couple of hours I'd spend in church. But the three of us had one moment of bliss—going out to pick blackberries.

We'd wander down the two-lane curvy mountain road with our empty milk jugs in hand. We each had one. The top was cut off back to the handle. The swoop of the opening was small enough to keep us from losing any **blackberries once** the jug was full. It took a lot of blackberries to fill a gallon jug.

At first, Martha was reluctant to let us out of her sight, but we convinced her that we were making money off the blackberries—money for her. She was the main beneficiary of all our hard work, but that didn't bother us because the blackberries gave us an escape from reality and drew us closer.

We tried to pick as many gallons of blackberries as we could so we could sell them to buy school supplies. I didn't want much—some pencils, a backpack, and a notebook to call my own so I wouldn't have to keep asking if I could borrow a piece of paper. These tiny things gave me a sense of normalcy when I opened my locker. They made me feel like I fit in with the other students.

During those blackberry years, the three of us ranged between eleven and thirteen years old. We'd challenge each other to find the biggest and best patches. The more berries we saw, the more excitement we felt. Where we lived, we had so many options to go picking. Some days we

Blackberries come part and parcel with the worst days of my life as well as the moment I escaped.

would venture off to the field adjacent from the trailer park and find ourselves on neighbors' properties.

At first we would hear, "Get off this land," or "You're not welcome here." One of the neighbors finally got used to seeing us climb up and down his fence and run through his open field. He must have seen something in us or admired how hard we worked, because whenever he saw us he took the time to talk to us and ask why we were collecting his beautiful blackberries. I think he took pity on us when we told him it was to buy school supplies. He started asking if we wanted anything to drink or eat. To me, this was the blackberry bonanza.

This soon became our favorite spot. We loved climbing over the rustic white fence, running through the tall grass that brushed up to our knees, and dodging the stunning horses that galloped through the field.

Some days, we would hunt for blackberries along the curvy, busy mountain roads. We watched out for each other and made sure none of us got hit by a car. People driving by would see us, burrowed into those bushes, trying to get every last berry. Sometimes, we'd keep following the berries and suddenly end up miles from the trailer park. We'd have to navigate our way back home in the dark with only the moon to guide us.

Sometimes, we'd just run through the woods, catching a glimpse of the sun's rays peeking through the tall white oak trees. We'd splash each other when we ran through those ice-cold streams. I can still hear our laughter and the echoes of our voices in the woods. It was an adventure, but it was also part of **our survival.**

Over the years, we became friends with our neighbors in the trailer park. Sometimes we'd sneak out of one trailer and camp out in another. For us, it was fun and cool to see how "normal" people lived.

Then, every once in a while, we'd see the sheriff's car circling up the gravel road headed up toward our trailer. Every time I saw the blue, white, and red lights come around the corner to enter the park, I would hold my breath. Is today the day they're coming for us? Is today the day I finally get to breathe?

Is today the day they're coming for us?

Sometimes the neighbors called them after hearing Martha's screechy voice resonating through the park as she yelled at us or after seeing the abuse marks on our faces, arms, legs, and backs. A polite woman who looked like she was dressed in her Sunday best always accompanied the nice sheriff.

It was the same story every time. "We had a call regarding some type of abuse going on here." Or, "We received a call that Martha was hitting her children again," the sheriff would say. They'd interview Martha alone, sitting at the kitchen table. Once they wrapped up the conversation with her, it was our turn. Sometimes they questioned us together, sometimes individually. Every time the sheriff asked, "Are you okay?" We knew our one and only response had better be "yes", because we knew the moment they left we would be greeted by the back of Martha's hand if we said anything else.

One particular sunny day felt different. I don't know why this day had an edge to it, but for some reason, I felt shattered. I felt deserted. I felt suffocated. I felt like a punching bag that was running out of the capacity for new distress. Every single part of me hurt. My head hurt the worst because it was Martha's favorite target when she punished me.

I was thirteen and up super early in the morning, doing my mile-long housekeeping To Do list: sweeping, mopping, dusting, and doing the dishes. I remember every little detail about that day. How I couldn't find all the dirty dishes because there were so many scattered around the house. I remember the small metal sink filled with Dawn soapsuds. How I couldn't stand the shape of Martha's miserable face. How I couldn't stand anything at all about the trailer. How I happened to glance up from the sink to find Martha's wrinkly fingers wrapped tightly around my sister's tiny neck while she pushed her into the couch. Watching my sister desperately gasp for air broke my paralysis.

At that moment, something in me just snapped. I knew something needed to happen, and happen fast. I stood there, scrubbing a cast iron skillet and I knew, just knew, that this unhappy, emotionless, fuming, wretched woman who was theoretically my grandmother was going to end up killing one of us someday. Or worse, I'd turn on her and give her a taste of her own medicine and end up in jail myself.

I dropped the pan into the sink and dashed out of the screen door. I ran, as hard and fast as I could, to the first trailer I could see. Tears streamed down my cheeks and the wind tangled in my hair. I could feel the tall green grass brushing against my bare feet.

This was the day. The day things *were* going to change.

I slung open the screen door of a dirty white and green trailer and started knocking. The knocking turned into pounding, louder and heavier with every thud from my fist. As soon as the door opened, I ran inside, screaming for the elderly woman who lived there to help me call the Department of Social Services.

I started to panic while I waited for the woman to find the number. What was Martha doing right now? Was she beating my brother? My sister? Was she coming after me?

And then, the phone was in my hand and there was a soft voice on the other end saying, "How can I help you?"

All I could do was cry. Cry for help—for my brother and sister and me. "My brother, sister, and me are in bad shape. We need help. Tomorrow, we'll be on the mountain road picking blackberries. Please pick us up. Please come get us. Please save us."

Please come get us. Please save us.

Chapter 3

Bags

*T*he next morning the sun was trying to peek through the short green floral curtains in between gusts of wind that waved the curtains in and out. I lay in my bed and watched them for a long time, hoping and praying that today was the day.

My heart hammered in my chest, as if I was still talking on the phone in the neighbor's kitchen. They had promised they would come for us, but that would only happen if I got up and pretended today was an ordinary day. Martha still didn't know I'd called social services, but I was terrified she'd find out and beat me.

My siblings had no idea what would happen when we headed out with our gallon jugs in tow to find blackberries. But I knew, and it was a sweet secret I held tight in my chest.

While we pulled blackberries off the bushes on the side of that curvy mountain road, a maroon 1990 Ford Taurus passed us a couple of times. I didn't think much about it. After a third lap around, the car stopped along the shoulder, wheels half on the grass and half on the hot pavement. The driver's door opened and out stepped a woman in a dark navy pantsuit. We were on opposite sides of the road. Her eyes met mine and my breath caught. She yelled, "I'm Mary Davis with the Department of Social Services. Are you Elizabeth?"

I froze. I knew that the good Lord above had sent this kind lady to rescue my siblings and me. All I had to do was move. Cross the street. Say yes.

I nodded and she came to us. My siblings were confused, but we followed her across the road. She pulled out a brown clipboard with a fresh sheet of notebook paper tacked to the top. "I'm here to take you into foster care."

I had no idea what foster care was or what was about to come, but I knew it had to be better than this horrible life we had been living. Holding hands, we all piled into the back seat. Then Mary drove us back to the trailer.

I was scared. What if Martha put up a fight again? What if Mary believed Martha, like the sheriff always did? We all hopped out of the car, following behind Mary like she was a mother goose and we were her goslings.

Martha stood in the kitchen, the Marlboro in her right hand dropping ash on the linoleum floor. "Who are you?" Anger flooded her face.

I don't remember all the details of that day. I remember Mary introducing herself and saying she was here to take us. I remember Mary telling us to pack our bags while she argued with Martha.

And I remember running through the hallway with my arms full of the few shirts, shoes, and pants I owned, along with a single stuffed bear. I started to cry, not because I was sad to be leaving but because I was getting out of that abyss of pain and neglect. My siblings and I were leaving. Finally.

I looked in the storage closet to find a bag but all I saw was a pile of bright orange bags. They were sturdy and thick, the kind made for the State Department for prisoners to fill with trash and debris from the side of the road.

My belongings only filled the bottom of the bag. I did one final sweep of the trailer to make sure I wasn't leaving any part of me behind and then I slung the bag over my shoulder. As I was about to open the front door to step towards my future, Martha groused, "Where do you think you're going, young lady?"

I sat my orange trash bag on the stained tan carpet. "What are you talking about?"

"You're not going anywhere. That woman can take your brother and sister, but you're staying right here with me."

I quaked at the sound of her voice. Then I suddenly realized everything had changed, so I let her words literally go in one ear and out the other. I picked up my trash bag, took one look at her and said, "The only people I've ever loved just walked out this front door. I'm going where they are." And I walked out of that single-wide trailer for the last time.

I settled into the backseat of the Taurus with my siblings and watched as we pulled away. Martha stood in her driveway, still holding her cigarette, shocked and mad—and finally in our past. I took a big deep breath and smiled. I didn't know where we were going and I didn't know what the future held. I really didn't care, as long as it involved the three of us.

After what seemed like a thirty-minute car ride, we finally pulled into this big, almost empty parking lot adjacent to a big brick building. We sat there for a while, in a space that wasn't surrounded by other cars.

After a few minutes, another car pulled up beside us. Mary rolled down her window and started talking to the man in the next car over. After a little while, the man got out and opened the back door of his car. He then walked over and opened the back door to our car and asked my brother to step out.

"What's going on?" I said. "Where are you taking him?" They didn't answer me. My brother got into the other car. Alone. With his bag.

I felt paralyzed. I didn't get to say anything to my brother. I didn't get to give him a hug, I didn't get to tell him goodbye, and I didn't get to tell him I loved him. Nothing. Not a single word. Just silence and mistrust. The last image I remember was of him looking out the car's rear window while it seemed to evaporate as the man drove away, with a piece of me sitting in the back seat.

I kept wondering where we were going. Was another car coming to take my sister away, too? I had no idea what was going on. What was supposed to be something wonderful had quickly become frightening and sad. What had I done? I thought I had made the right choice. If I had known that they were going to separate us, I wouldn't have called for help. I would've stayed in that trailer and suffered Martha's wrath as long as it meant we were all together.

I still had my sister with me, at least for the moment. All I could do was hold on to those moments and cherish them because I didn't know how long we would be together or when I would see her again.

The man drove away, with a piece of me sitting in the back seat.

Sometime, late in the evening, after what seemed like an eternity, we finally pulled up to another big building. Mary put the car in park, gathered up her things, then stepped out of the car and opened the back door for us. "We've arrived."

"Arrived?" I asked. "Where are we?"

"We are at a group home in North Carolina." She nodded toward the bags. "Both of you grab your things and come with me."

"Group home?" I thought. "What the heck is that?" I looked down at my orange trash bag, still clutched tightly in my right hand. I hadn't let go of it since we left Martha's. It was all I had to identify who I was.

Then I realized Mary had said the word "both". That meant my sister and I would be together, at least for now. Whatever the situation we were about to walk into might be, I knew we would be okay and tackle it as a team.

The group home was different than I imagined. When my sister and I walked through those double doors, Mary introduced us to our new house parents and then escorted us straight to our room. Mary didn't stay long, and after she left I wasn't sure if I would ever see her again. I wasn't really sure about anything. This was all new territory.

More than 260,000 children enter foster care every year.

I kept wondering about my brother. Where was he?

Was he also in a group home? Was he alone? Would I eventually be able to talk to him?

The bedroom my sister and I were put in was pretty much a room filled with emptiness. There were two twin mattresses that sat on wooden frames, each with two drawers underneath. In the right corner of the room was an old beat up chest of drawers with random names of previous misplaced foster children on the drawers, some carved into the wood, some written in black marker. Since we all shared one bed at Martha's, having our own bed was kind of a big deal and something I knew I would need to grow accustomed to. We were finally able to have our own space.

Once I was in that room with my sister, I finally let go of the grip I had on my trash bag. I laid it on my new bed and emptied out the contents, then took my time placing the only pieces of clothing I owned into one of the drawers under the bed. I set my favorite bear on my pillow.

It took my sister and me a little time to muster up the courage to leave our new room and walk out into the dayroom to meet our other housemates. The living room had a huge blue leather couch in one corner and a sofa that looked big enough to hold ten people. A scarred wooden coffee table with a small television sitting on it sat across the room. The walls were empty. No pictures, no art, no drawings—nothing. The kitchen was just as ordinary and impersonal. Pots and pans hung from the ceiling over a long stainless steel island. The refrigerator sat against the far wall, but what I noticed most was it wasn't padlocked.

I was relieved just knowing we would be able to eat. I was used to sharing things with other people, so that part didn't bother me. The group home might not be so bad. When I went to bed that night, I looked over at my sister in the other bed. She smiled. I smiled. We had each other, at least. All was good in the world.

That peace only lasted a week. One day, Mary returned to the group home. At first, I was happy to see her—until I heard her say, "I'm here for Elizabeth."

I ran over to her. "I'm here!"

She told me to get my things. I asked her why and then asked if I should tell my sister to get hers, too.

"No, only yours," Mary shook her head and shrugged. As I started to head down the hallway to my room, I had the same gut feeling I got when my brother was whisked away. I pulled out my trash bag and began to pack.

By the time my sister walked into the room, I couldn't even see what I was doing because I was crying so hard. "She came for me and not you," I wept. The two of us stood in the hallway for a long time, crying and holding on to each other.

At this point, I wasn't sure where I was going or why my sister wasn't going with me. I didn't know anything. At least I got to say goodbye and tell my sister that I loved her. As Mary opened up the back door to that same Taurus, I turned around to give my sister one last hug. Then off we went, leaving the group home and one more thing I knew behind.

Years later, my sister and I were placed in the same foster home for a little while and I eventually got to see my brother from afar when we both wound up at a different group home. I don't think he ever knew I was there, but I happened to catch a glimpse of him playing outside on the basketball court. I've always known those momentary glimpses were the good Lord's way to show me my brother was doing okay. Of course, this was long before social media and texting, so communication between us was scarce.

The worst part was the distance in my mind. The further apart I got from them, the more they felt like a memory. I wondered about them all the time—about whether they were happy and if they were being treated well. My brother and sister were my life and the only thing that felt like home.

As I moved from one place to another, I felt lost, empty and disconnected. Disconnected from a world that was supposed to be easier after living with Martha's wrath. Disconnected from my family. Disconnected from who I was.

> As I moved from one place to another, I felt lost, empty and disconnected.

Over the next five years, I lived or visited about ten foster and group homes, some for a short while and others for a bit longer. I went to at least three different schools and shared my time with so many random people they could circle the globe if they all held hands.

One thing stayed the same—every time I moved to a new home, I never fully unpacked. I always made sure my bag was ready because I never knew where the next knock on the door would take me.

At any given time almost a half a million children are in foster care.

Chapter 4

Nametags

The small town of Andrews, North Carolina is a quaint and vibrant place tucked away in the foothills of the Great Smoky Mountains. It is punctuated by a couple of red lights, old brick buildings that date back decades, and some of the most kindhearted individuals one could ever meet. It's a small town in every sense of the word—my graduation class was less than seventy students. It was a lovely place for my last foster home, but the journey there was very rough.

In the years after the woman from social services picked us up on the side of the road and took us out of that terrible existence, I was introduced to many families and ways of life. Some families were nice and open to the idea of having a child that was not theirs in their home, while others were the opposite. The worst of my foster homes felt like I was living at Martha's all over again.

So many of the foster parents I stayed with had no interest in the children living in their home. They would hibernate in their bedrooms, watching TV while their foster kids fended for themselves. One particular home I stayed in took in more kids than I could count. It was so crowded that every night I had to find a new place to lay my head—on the couch or the floor, or the top or lower bunk. Families like them weren't fostering for the right reasons; they did it for the money. It's sad that some people take advantage of a vulnerable situation.

Not all foster homes were bad. On a couple of occasions I stayed at respite homes, where kids leaving their current home were placed with another family for the weekend. Many of these families were well off and treated the kids well. I often didn't feel good enough to go on their outings and vacations. Most of the time, the families I stayed with didn't bother to get to know me, but some of the respite homes were different. One family owned an ice cream shop and spent a lot of time with me. On my rare respite stays with them, which happened every couple of months, they allowed me the opportunity to make some pocket change and work the register. I was very grateful for the opportunity because it kept my mind busy and made me feel needed.

Andrews, however, was the town where my life as an adult would officially begin. It seemed like previous years all passed in a blur, although they had been filled with upheaval and changes that came as frequently as the seasons. I didn't think about the future when I first entered foster care, and I never thought about what would happen when I aged out of the system.

After reaching the age of 18, 20% of the children who were in foster care will become instantly homeless.

Aging out sounds like I hit retirement or something, but all I had to do was turn eighteen and I was on my own. Literally. In the foster care system, there's an expiration date on your life. When you hit it, those random strangers you've grown to rely on throw you to the wolves and tell you to try and survive this thing called life. The closer I got to my eighteenth birthday, the more questions I had about the unknown: *Where will I go? Where will I stay? How will I pay my bills? How will I afford a car or car insurance? What will happen to me if I don't succeed out in the world on my own?*

And then the day came. I was eighteen. I'd graduated high school and I was officially an adult. I literally felt like I had to grow up so fast my childhood years were just a delusion.

I was out of the system and no longer the responsibility of my foster parents, but I wasn't completely on my own—I had an assigned independent living counselor who gave me a monthly stipend from the state, an amount less than thirteen hundred dollars. The counselor was there to help me navigate my confusing new world, but on a limited basis. Thankfully, I also had the support of my foster parents. They could have just said goodbye and shown me the door after my birthday, but the Millers were the kindest and sweetest foster parents I ever had.

While I lived with them, they not only provided me with a place to stay, but they also restored my faith. Mr. Miller was a pastor at the local Church of God in that quaint small town. There was just something about him that made me enjoy sitting on that squeaky front pew of the white church with the red door, listening to him talk about God. Perhaps he reminded me of Martha's father and the silence of unspoken words, or maybe it was just Mr. Miller's kind, soft voice.

Mrs. Miller was the type of pastor's wife who always had a smile on her face. She made sure their church family was taken care of and even though I was no longer in their home, she made sure I was taken care of too. The Millers helped me with a few basic necessities like a bed, a set of dishes, and a couple of towels and washcloths.

I moved into a four-hundred-square foot apartment that smelled like mothballs. It neighbored a shopping center and wasn't much, but it was mine. I had almost nothing to fill those empty rooms, but what I did have was my very own. This tiny apartment was my space to breathe and finally unpack my bags.

I thought I'd have my counselor and foster family to rely on indefinitely but it only lasted for a short while, and a few months later my communication with that sweet foster family slowly came to an end.

Only 1 out of every 2 foster kids who age out of the system will have some form of gainful employment by the age of 24.

In the years since, whenever I visit the area, I stop by and take the time to catch up.

Truly alone for the first time, I was very naïve. Anyone who offered to be my friend, I just assumed they were. H.G. Bohn once said, "An idle brain is the devil's workshop," and in those months I filled my mind and my loneliness with other people. I ended up hanging out with the wrong kind of people. They were a means to an end, a way to ease the emptiness running through my veins. It wasn't long before I recognized this was not the life I wanted to live. I didn't want to become one of those kids—the ones in foster care who escape their lives through drugs or alcohol or sex. I wanted more, and I didn't want my past to define my existence.

The best part of that tiny little apartment was my name on the door. I would come home and look at the mail, or at the nametag by the doorbell, and realize that was my name. Mine. All those years spent in foster care, I rarely saw my name on anything other than the documents that floated around with me while I transitioned from one home to another, or on prescription bottles approved by one of the many therapists that I met along the way. When I was part of the system, I'd always felt like my name was unimportant. I was just another foster kid—to the government, to most of the families that took me in, and to the new schools I started every few months.

I got my first job at fifteen. I remember the first time I swiped my nametag through the time clock at Hardee's. Pride flooded me, and I almost wanted to swipe it again just to see my name flash on the screen. To me, that moment was one of my greatest accomplishments.

I didn't have a penny in my pocket, didn't know a thing about customer service, but I did know how to push a button and fill a cup with ice and soda. Working there made me curious about how things functioned. I also became ambitious for more. I wanted to move up from being a cashier to cooking in the back, to working the drive-thru window, or to cleaning the customer area. It didn't matter what job I did—the sense of pride I felt doing the work was so satisfactory.

I'm not really sure why all these things had me so thrilled when I was that age. Maybe it filled a void in me, that feeling of being wanted. Hardee's needed me, the customers needed me, and I needed them. For once, I felt like this was where I belonged.

As the years progressed, so did my collection of nametags. I began working at Popeye's, then McDonald's. It seemed like I had hit every fast food restaurant in that quaint little town. Each place was unique in its own way and brought out a different side of me. I was like a caterpillar in its different stages of development. I was a bit shy, timid and ashamed at first, but over time I started to find myself and came out of my chrysalis.

I was like a caterpillar in its different stages of development.

As soon as I began living on my own, I thought about my future; one that went beyond working in fast food places and having a real career. I didn't want my education to end with just a high school diploma. I began researching my options and soon found Tri-County Community College, a small campus about a thirty-minute car ride from where I lived. I wasn't sure how I was going to pay for an education or how I was going to make it to classes and juggle a job, but I was determined to make it happen.

I applied for any type of assistance I could find: Pell Grants, Perkins Loans, financial aid, and so on. The application and approval process was intense and stressful. I religiously checked my mailbox several times a day, both scared and nervous. I never wanted anything more in my life to happen than this.

The day that envelope arrived in my mailbox I stopped and held my breath until I had the courage to open it. There they were, on a sheet of paper below my name, the words I'd prayed for: *Tri-County Community College would like to officially accept you into the Associate of Arts program*. I began to cry, filled with a sense of accomplishment. I couldn't believe it. I was going to college!

There is less than a 3% chance for children who have aged out of foster care to earn a college degree at any point in their life.

My life was still far from perfect, but it was my own. My apartment didn't have much furniture, but it was just enough for me. I was thankful to have my own space—a space no one could come and take me away from. My couch was a couple of beach folding chairs, which were eventually replaced by a used futon. I couldn't afford cable, but settled for the three channels I could pick up occasionally on a small Samsung TV with a built-in VHS. Most of the time I would make up a pallet of blankets on the living room floor and fall asleep to Trace Adkins or George Strait. I was too afraid to sleep in the bed in the back room. Maybe because it was officially the first time I lived by myself and not surrounded by foster parents, foster children, or Martha.

When the holidays approached and I had nowhere to go, I sought solace by sleeping under my Christmas tree, using its colorful lights as comfort on some of my darkest nights. Many times I just lay there wondering where my sister and brother were. I would've given anything in those moments to hear their voices. The thought of seeing them one day gave me hope.

I knew I had to learn how to budget, so when I began to figure out my bills and all that entailed, I realized I was clueless about anything having to do with finances. I didn't have a bank account, credit cards, or any place to save my hard-earned money. So, I opened a checking account and, like with everything else, I was amazed to see my name and address on those slips of paper. This was me—where I lived, who I was. For as long as I wanted it to be.

The problem? I didn't know how to write a check. I knocked on my neighbor's door. I was embarrassed and hesitated a second before asking her to help me. I expected her to think I was crazy or to laugh at me. Instead, she smiled. "Absolutely, Elizabeth, I would be happy to help you." Even today, I think of her when I look at my checkbook.

So many people helped me along the way in those first difficult years. When I needed to get a new car and didn't have sufficient credit, I asked my hairdresser if she would mind co-signing for me and she did. When I needed advice about my car, health, or just day-to-day living, I asked people I worked with. I sought guidance and gained confidence from strangers, when most people would normally ask their parents or extended family. I was trying to do whatever it took to survive and find some sort of normalcy in my crazy world. I was putting the pieces together of who I was, one moment at a time.

> I was putting the pieces together of who I was, one moment at a time.

I didn't have a lot of tangible belongings to hang on to, but I knew there was one thing I did have that no one could take away from me—my faith. I knew that as long as I believed, I would be able to overcome every challenge thrown my way. Including finding my true identity.

Like most kids growing up in the world of foster care, I was labeled: foster kid, orphan, worthless, dumb, etc. Society put labels on us, sorted us into folders and cases, and over the years I started to feel like I wasn't anything other than those labels.

I have saved most of my nametags over the years. I was so proud to escape that label and to have an identity. It wasn't perfect but it was mine. Who could know that the next nametag I added to my collection would set off a chain of events that would forever change my life.

Chapter 5

Strangers

One beautiful summer morning, I woke up with tons of enthusiasm to start a brand new day at a brand new job as a sales associate. My days spent working long hours and coming home smelling like grease were finally over. I traded in my short sleeve button-down collared shirt with the Golden Arches logo for a vibrant royal blue vest smock top with the words, "How may I help you?" emblazoned on it. I didn't know much about the Walmart Supercenter Store #0515, located in Murphy, North Carolina, nor did I know a single person in that enormous store, but I was excited about my new adventure all the same.

I started out as a cashier, and people from different walks of life came wandering through my line. Some wanted to stay and chat awhile, while others were ready to get on their way. No matter how I felt, I always greeted and thanked each customer with a smile. I wondered where all these people were going and where they came from. They all had histories, families, connections, while the little bit of a family I had was scattered in the wind.

I never had any problems meeting people, maybe because foster kids are always having to talk to random people. So to me, it was normal. Besides, I was always a talker, but I'd freeze up when it came to certain subjects. Questions like, *where are you from* or *what was your family like? Do you have any siblings? Do you have any plans for the holidays?* Those questions made me feel unsure how to answer, and embarrassed that I couldn't seem to figure out how to respond. Instead, I would change the subject.

One day, I spent hours working on the floor with a fellow associate organizing the shelves. All that time together led to a lot of conversation, and at some point I opened up about who I was and where I came from. We parted ways after chatting for what seemed like forever and a day. I hardly knew this person, but deep down I wanted to thank her for taking the time to have an open and honest conversation with me.

From that day forward, it was as if a wall had come down. That conversation led to another and then another. Before I knew it, everyone I worked with knew I was more than just a name on a nametag. I went from feeling like something smaller than the head of a pin in this broad universe to feeling like I was part of something greater. Friendships started to blossom with people of all ages, from nineteen to

I went from feeling like something smaller than the head of a pin in this broad universe to feeling like I was part of something greater.

ninety-nine. Associates became friends and those friendships turned into family. I went from being alone during holidays, to being offered a seat at many dinner tables. I would stay so often at some friends' houses they set up a bedroom just for me. For the first time in my life, people who said they were my "friends" really were. These people had my back, no matter what, and were always there to pick me up whenever I fell.

For me, the hardest part of growing up without a family wasn't the fact that I didn't have someone telling me they loved me, the stability of staying in one home, or to not have someone to call Mom and Dad. And it wasn't that I didn't have aunts, uncles, or cousins, or a family pet. It was not having grandparents.

Maybe it came from watching too much television, but I always wanted to have a middle name that belonged to "grandma" or to carry around a black and white faded photo of both of my "grandparents" in my wallet. I wanted to have "grandma's" favorite recipes to try and replicate and fail at making because mine would never taste as good as hers. I wanted to go to "grandma's" house so she could comfort me in ways Mom and Dad could not. I always wanted to sit in a rocker and listen to stories my "grandpa" would share of his good ol' days and time spent at war. I didn't have any of that—until I met Carl and Joy.

As the months passed, Walmart began to feel like more than just a place where I spent eight hours a day scanning items, restocking shelves, and changing truck tires. To me, it was beginning to feel like a place I could call home. These were my people. People who didn't judge me because I came from a past over which I had no control, who didn't see me as a person without parents—to them, I was just "Liz". The people I worked with did whatever they could to make a difference in my young life. I found myself dreading the end of my shift and made any and every excuse to stay a tad longer. I walked around asking associates if I could take over their shifts. I wasn't ready to leave the place I felt the most at home to go and sleep in a home that was full of empty space. These associates weren't just coworkers, they were my family.

Carl was a delicate, elderly man who worked as a greeter. He greeted every person with a smile from him and, "Good afternoon, welcome to Walmart." His face was lined, and to me it seemed as if those lines

> These associates weren't just coworkers, they were my family.

held the secrets of his life. I thought how lucky his grandchildren were to have him as a grandpa.

We became friends and, a little at a time, Carl helped fill some of the emptiness in my shattered heart. We spent many of our short breaks sitting on the cold vanilla-colored plastic chairs that occupied the break room in the back of the store, talking up a storm. Some days, I would just sit and listen to him share stories over a warm cup of coffee, and sometimes I asked him for advice. He began to feel like my "grandpa".

Joy was a petite, elderly woman with long, straight, snow-white hair who worked in the fabrics department. She looked like the ideal grandmother—her hair up in a bun, held in place with bejeweled combs, her makeup perfect, and a sweater with every outfit. We would laugh, cry, and chat over rolls of yarn, fabric, and a plethora of sewing pins. She began to feel like my "grandma".

One of my friends at work, Roxy, knew how tight my finances were. After paying for school and rent, I was literally "robbing Peter to pay Paul" to pay the other bills and putting most of them on credit cards. I worked overtime but I could never seem to get ahead. Out of the blue, she offered me a room in her ranch-style house. I hesitated, unsure if I wanted to give up the first place that was truly mine. My haven. But the numbers won out. I was a year away from earning my Associate of Arts degree from Tri-County Community College and could use the financial break to help me regain my focus and get that diploma.

I lived there for a few months before she and her husband took new jobs in another state. I opted to stay in North Carolina, even though it meant I would be homeless. I crashed on friends' couches and slept in my car many, many nights, trying to save money for first, last, and security, so I could afford those last few months of school.

Not having a home made me sort of feel like and item someone returns to the customer service desk at Walmart. When someone purchases an item and it doesn't fit their needs, they return it and either choose something else or say goodbye forever to the original item. There was no emotional connection to the crockpots and shirts people returned; they were just things they didn't want in their house anymore. That's pretty much how I felt my life had been, shuffled from place to place where people didn't really invest in me emotionally. Living with Martha and then in and out of multiple foster homes, and now I was jumping from place to place. Although I didn't come with a price tag, I still felt like I was being returned quiet often.

One day, while working the customer service desk, I met a woman named Evelyn. She and I exchanged small talk and worked side-by-side helping customers. When I finally caught a break from the long line of returns, I took a personal call.

One of my best friends who worked at Walmart asked me a simple question—*how are you?*

Everything poured out of me; the move to the ranch house with Roxy, then staying with friend after friend, and even sleeping many nights in my car. I was exhausted and stressed, and I began to cry. I hung up the phone and stood there weeping. I knew I still carried my faith around in my back pocket and that I was now, more than ever, relying heavily on it, but I felt so lost and alone right then. I called out to God, pleading for help. I asked Him to show me a sign, any kind of sign that I would be all right.

Then I composed myself and walked back to my station. Evelyn came up to me and apologized for eavesdropping. "I couldn't help but overhear you," she said, "and I know you don't really know me, but I wanted to let you know that you're more than welcome to come stay with me and my husband. We have a furnished basement and you can have it rent-free until you get back on your feet." Before I could protest, she held up her hand. "I already called my husband to stop by here so you could meet him. We both want you to move into that space."

I was speechless and couldn't speak for a long time. There I was, living out of my car one minute

> I asked Him to show me a sign, any kind of sign that I would be all right.

and the next I'm offered a free new home with complete strangers. But were they really strangers? Perhaps they were my guardian angels, planted by God after my prayer.

I'm not sure how long I stood there with tears streaming down my cheeks before I accepted her offer. "Yes," I answered in little more than a whisper. I was so afraid to count on this, to believe in it.

After my shift ended, I met them at a little ice cream shop down the road. We ended up having one of the best conversations I'd ever had in my entire life, and through that I gained a better understanding of who they were. As I sat there talking with them, I had spiritual chills (goosebumps) up and down my arms and legs. The feeling was beyond amazing. I knew, right then and there, that the good Lord was with me and the sign I had been praying for was sitting right across from me—Evelyn and Gene.

That night, I unloaded my car and moved into their basement apartment. A home. I had a home again. In all honesty, I'm not really sure how my life would've turned out if it weren't for the amazing strangers I met at Walmart Superstore #0515. They took a chance on a girl without a family, and their love and grace changed my life in a thousand ways. For that, and for them, I will always be grateful.

Chapter 6
The Club

I thought about them all the time, every morning and night. I hadn't seen my sister in eight years and only saw my brother once in passing. The day we were pulled out of our hell with Martha and sent to different foster care homes, the Department of Social Services assured me— over and over again—that I would get to see my siblings. We'd have open lines of communications, like letters and telephone conversations.

None of that ever happened.

I lay awake at night grateful for my life, but at the same time worried about my brother and sister. What kind of life were they leading? Were they okay, or did they get stuck in a worse situation than what we had left? I prayed for them all the time and prayed, if it was meant to be, that God would direct me back to my brother and sister one day.

I was only supposed to live with Evelyn and Gene for a short while, but I spent several happy years in that basement apartment. The sacrificial gesture of this kind couple left an everlasting impact on my exhausted soul. They had their own children and individual worries, but they always made sure I was included as part of the family. I truly thank them for that. With their support, I graduated with my Associate of Arts degree from Tri-County Community College and did so with grace and pride. Once I had a taste of what a true education felt like, I knew I wanted more.

7 out of 10 girls who age out of the foster care system will become pregnant before the age of 21.

While I always had a place to stay with Evelyn and Gene, I knew it would be a long time before I would be able to live completely on my own again; at least not with my meager income. I was working three jobs while trying to get through school. They graciously told me to stay as long as I needed, but I really wanted to find a way to afford a room in the dorm so I could have the same experience as millions of other college kids.

I started applying, every application was sent wrapped in a downpour of feelings. I wasn't just going to school, I was doing it with the security of a roof over my head and knowing where my next meal would come from.

Then the acceptance letter from Western Carolina University arrived. I was thrilled, then I panicked. How was I going to pay for this with only fifty dollars in my bank account? Jack made it his mission to set aside his valuable time on a daily basis to surf the web on his old Hewlett Packard desktop, looking for any type of financial assistance or scholarships available to foster children. Gene's dogged search eventually landed upon a small outreach program: Orphan Foundation of America. Between their support and the help of financial aid, my college tuition and fees were covered.

On move-in day at Western Carolina University, my stomach was filled with butterflies. I drove up a curvy rural road tucked away in the heart of a mountain, thinking of very different curved road and how much my life had changed since that day I was picking blackberries with my brother and sister. Again, I wondered where they were, if they were happy, and if they ever wondered about me.

When I saw the bronze Catamount statue, I knew I'd arrived at college. Even though it was a smaller campus, it seemed pretty gargantuan to me. I wasn't in that two red-light small town anymore. I drove several laps around the campus and then found my dormitory. I parked my car and sat there a moment, admiring the scenery around me.

Looking around, I saw families helping to carry boxes into their freshman's new dorm room.

I saw families wiping away tears of joy as they said goodbye. I saw families embraced in hugs so tight that you couldn't pull them apart if you wanted to.

I was alone. No family to say goodbye to, no mother to remind me to go to bed early and no father to tell me he was proud of me. There was no one to hug; no one but me.

"Liz," I whispered to myself, "I'm really proud of you for beginning the next chapter in your life, all on your own." Life had dealt me some pretty harsh blows, but stepping through the doors of those historic brick dorms was the hardest. That day, all I wanted was to have what every other person wanted on that day—someone to be proud of me.

> There was no one to hug; no one but me.

I didn't know a single soul on campus, but that was okay. My life was built on a foundation of strangers. It didn't take me as long as it did my roommate to become accustomed to life in the dorm. I was used to sharing my space with others, so having someone else in the small dorm room didn't bother me. I was, however, skeptical about getting close to my roommate. I wasn't sure if she was going to be around long. For the longest time, I kept comparing dorm life to the life I lived in foster care. How long was I going to be there? How often would I be getting a new roommate? Everything felt temporary.

It took a few months to fine-tune my major and minor, sift through the ups and downs of my class schedule, get my dorm room situated to fit my personality, and decide on the type of work-study program I wanted to try, yet I quickly discovered my love for school. I got into a groove, juggling parties with college friends, and strived for straight As.

Thursday nights were always set aside for "friends' night". My friends at school made every moment that much more gratifying. I'm a firm believer in having a good balance in your life. After a solid week of waking up early, sweaty runs between classes, massive note taking, and late-night study sessions at the library, my friends and I needed one night just for fun. Our typical go-to spot was a club located in the core of Maggie Valley, North Carolina. It was roughly two hours one way, but the time passed quickly in a car full of women who were ready for a few hours of dancing, singing, and mingling.

That night, the club was packed tighter than a Victorian era corset. I'd been drinking a little and dancing a lot, and as I turned to swing my long hair into a bun, I noticed a familiar face. My breath caught and I did a double take. One glance was all it took. I recognized the shape of her face, the sound of her laughter, and the color of her hair.

The young woman standing ten feet away from me was my long-lost sister.

I'd had a couple of cosmopolitans, and for a second I thought my eyes were playing tricks on me. What were the chances it was her? Eight long years of living apart and we end up at the same dance club?

I shoved my way through the crowd to get to her.

"Hey, I'm your sister, Elizabeth." I yelled, but my voice got lost in the blaring music, my words mixing with the songs until you couldn't tell them apart. She looked confused and didn't really respond. Maybe she thought I was just an acquaintance of a friend at the club instead of her actual sibling. She was surrounded by a group of her own people and I didn't want to say or do anything to make her uncomfortable, so I gave one of the girls in her group my phone number and asked if she would have my sister call me the next day.

When the bartender yelled, "Last call!" we said a short goodbye and I watched her disappear into the sea of college students. I headed back to my friends and we made the trek back over the mountain to our campus.

I couldn't sleep that night. I tossed and turned, trying to process what just happened. I wondered where she'd been for the past eight years. I worried that she wouldn't call me and that she would forget about me. I was fairly certain that running into me at the club triggered a past she longed to forget.

The next day, I was in my room studying when my phone rang. I didn't recognize the number, but knew it had to be her. "Hey Elizabeth, this is Melissa. How are you doing?"

Our conversation was too short, but she invited me to meet her the following Saturday. It turned out she lived only an hour and a half away.

My last memories of my sister were when we stayed in the same group home for one, too-brief week when I was thirteen. I had no expectations of how this would turn out but, like my life had always played out, I was just going to go with it.

My sister lived in a gray and white cottage house on a hill with a white paved driveway. At the door, I was immediately greeted by my sister, her friends, Janna and Shanna and their parents, Rhondi & Jif. They turned out to be my sister's adoptive family. They had met her by chance one day and brought her into their lives.

The number of foster kids who are eligible for adoption, on average, every year: 101,666.

They invited me in for coffee, and from that one invitation I now have a lifetime of memories. This extraordinary family had provided my sister with a stable foundation. While I was off living my own life, this family was making sure my sister was living hers. What Evelyn and Gene had done for me, this couple had done for my sister. I will be forever indebted to them for being the protectors my sister needed. I guess you could call them angels who walked amongst us.

As it turned out, my sister and I were attending the same college. This had to be God's work. He not only sent her to Western Carolina, but to that club last week. Whatever had brought her back into my life, I was grateful. When God steps in, you should never question His intentions. Instead, be thankful for the new opportunity in your life.

Chapter 7
Newspapers

Guilt still consumed me.

I finally found my sister, but where was my brother? I couldn't get the image out of my head, him looking back at me through the dusty rear window of that Ford Taurus. While I was grateful to have my sister, I still felt empty. Life just wouldn't be complete until all three of us were together again.

By the middle of my junior year at Western Carolina University, I was knee-deep in living the dorm life. School was fantastic and the renewed relationship with my sister was starting to take off. Unfortunately, between our class schedules, demanding jobs, and the long, curvy roads between us, we didn't get to see each other that much, so we decided to move into an apartment off campus the next school year. I was excited to have this time to get closer to her. Eight years apart was a long time to make up for. For senior year, my sister, her two adoptive sisters and I rented a third-floor apartment less than a mile from campus. I was beyond elated to be under the same roof with my sister again. As my personal life began to get more settled, I started looking forward to life after college. I knew I was going to need a job and the best way to get one was through an internship. Internships are like bridges, providing college students with real-world scenarios to help them shift from student life to a professional career. I saw other students around me landing internships and began to doubt my abilities and myself. I wondered if foster kids were afforded the same opportunities.

One rainy Thursday morning, I was rushing to clean out my inbox and sent several emails to trash. I'm not sure I'll ever know why I decided to look through my trash bin, but I'm so glad I did. I spotted one with the subject line, "Orphan Foundation Of America Internship in Washington, DC." The same organization that helped fund my college education was offering an opportunity I desperately wanted. I completed the application and collected the required documents, then sucked in a deep breath and hit the send button.

The hours, days, and weeks that followed seemed to move at a snail's pace. There were times when I found myself clicking the refresh button over and over and over again. If there was a repeat button, I'm sure I would have put it to good use. I was looking for any response: good, mediocre, or bad; no matter what, I was prepared for it. My life had held so many disappointments that I told myself not to get my hopes up too high.

When I least expected it, I finally got their response. In big, bold print, it said: "Congratulations, you

> My life had held so many disappointments that I told myself not to get my hopes up too high.

have been selected for the Orphan Foundation of America 2004 Internship program." I nearly fell out of my chair.

The Orphan Foundation of America had such a major impact on my college success. Their stipend every semester not only contributed to my tuition and books, they helped me believe that I could do it. They gave me hope, purpose, and a chance at a good life. If you're looking for a worthwhile charity, consider them. They provide care and support for foster children everywhere who need that extra push toward their future.

In May of 2004, I proudly took the walk across the Western Carolina University stage and shook hands with all the professors, ending with my diploma for a major in Computer Information Systems and a minor in Criminal Justice. My smile was as wide as Texas.

A couple of days later, I packed my bags and boarded a plane for my first flight ever and headed to Washington, D.C. My six-week long paid internship included housing and meals. When I met the other recipients of the internship program, I realized that, for the first time in my life, I was with a group of people who all had something in common. We had all been foster kids, and all had our own stories. It didn't take long before we became fast friends and were all joined at the hip. We cooked meals, celebrated birthdays, and shared long talks around the picnic tables. Together. This group of friends soon turned into a family that shared a forever bond.

We each had our own assignments based on our majors. Some people worked at the state capitol while others worked at different jobs throughout the city. I ended up at Siemens Corporation, serving in a support role to various administrators and executives.

I loved working there. My experience at Siemens was like no other. Besides professional opportunities, I also had the good fortune to get glammed up from time to time and go to events at the Kennedy Center. I even met Angelina Jolie at the prescreening of the movie, *I Am David.* I got to take a comprehensive tour of the White House and sit at the conference table where hundreds of important decisions have been made. I felt like the queen of the city.

Near the end of my internship, I attended a fundraiser/advocacy event for the foundation. It was standing room only and people were packed in there like a can of sardines. I was in the same room as policy changers, curious citizens, and eager media, and had an opportunity to make my voice heard.

People around me asked state policy makers about things like Medicaid, changes to certain laws, or about state taxes. Then I heard my name. I hesitated. I wasn't prepared to stand in front of all those people and speak. I shuffled through the crowd. One of the politicians asked me, "If you could change one thing in your state, what would it be?"

In that moment, all I could think about was my brother. There I was, standing on one of the biggest platforms in the country, and I didn't hesitate for a minute. "If I could change one thing in my state, it would be to keep siblings together when they enter the foster care system," I said. "This is extremely important to me as I'm still searching for my brother, whom I haven't seen in thirteen years. He's the only other connection I have to my past." I'm sure I managed to mumble out a few more words after that, but they were mixed in with my tears.

I was stunned when the audience began to applaud. People who were sitting rose to their feet. I looked around and realized the entire room was clapping for me. Who knew my words could have so much power?

Reporters congregated around me and my Orphans of America friends sheltered me with warm hugs and lots of tissues. Having them there with me at that moment meant everything. They were the only people in the world who knew exactly how I felt.

A week after I got home from Washington, D.C., a reporter from the *Asheville Citizen-Times* newspaper showed up. They had heard about my story and wanted to write a feature on me.

A mixture of emotions ran through me: fear, anxiety, joy, and sorrow. My story was about to be out there for all to read and, for a moment, I felt ashamed. Then I realized that I had nothing to be ashamed of. This was my unique, twisted story and I was going to own it.

> My story was about to be out there for all to read and, for a moment, I felt ashamed.

After several interviews and a photo session with me, the story was published. I assumed it would be a small feature, buried back on page six. But no, it was right there on top of the fold, smack dab in the middle of the front page of the Sunday paper, and the story continued onto pages two and three. At the time, I had no idea how far that newspaper story would travel . . . until my phone rang two weeks later.

The Florida number was unfamiliar, so I sent it to voice mail. I played the message through my car speakers as I was driving. It was a woman from Florida Locators who had received the newspaper article and read it. "I have some news for you," she said.

After I heard the word "news" I knew I needed to pull off somewhere safe so I could make the return phone call—and it would change everything.

Chapter 8

Letters

*I*t took a long time to pry my fingers off the steering wheel and reach for my phone. I was terrified of what I would hear when I returned the call. I debated waiting a day or two, but the anticipation was too much to bear.

As soon as we dispensed with our hellos, the woman on the other end said, "We have located your brother, Matthew. He is living in New York City and seems to be doing fine." Thirteen years of wondering, crying, and hoping, had come to an end. He was alive and well. *There you go paying me a visit again, God.* I don't really remember the rest of our conversation. When I finally hung up, I sat there in my car for a long time, crying. This time they were not tears of fear or grief, but tears of joy. The thought of telling my sister, who had also worried and wondered about our brother, made me cry that much harder.

By the time I pulled into the driveway of our little brick house in Canton, North Carolina, I was so excited I nearly ran the car into the garage. I couldn't get into the house fast enough. It felt like my feet didn't hit the concrete walkway at all. As soon as I opened the door, I started calling for my sister. When she came downstairs, I told her to sit down because I had big news. She sank onto the couch, with Janna and Shanna beside her.

I took a deep breath and then told her what I knew about our brother. Like me, she was shocked for a moment and afraid to believe it was true. Then her shock turned to joy, then tears, then hugs.

Two weeks later, I finally talked to my brother. My sister and I made plans to fly to New York to see him. The *Asheville Citizen-Times* got wind of the latest story development and came by on the day we were leaving. It felt like the whole world was sitting on the edge of their seats waiting to see how my story would play out. The newspaper reporter asked questions and snapped pictures while my sister and I packed our bags and got ready for the reunion that had been more than ten years in the making.

We were both nervous; not just because of the trip, but because neither of us had ever been to New York. My only

There are 17,900,000 orphans who have lost both parents and are living in orphanages or on the streets around the world today.

experience with a big city was during my internship in Washington, D.C. A reporter from the *New York Times,* named Marie, met us at the gate. I knew how big of a deal this newspaper was, and to be approached by a reporter to talk about my story was pretty darn cool.

Marie, my sister, and I sat down in a little restaurant to do the interview. She had already talked to my brother and filled us in a little on his life. She said he was looking forward to seeing us, which was music to my ears. I was so happy to hear that he wanted to see us as badly as we wanted to see him. We wrapped up the conversation and our lunch, then my sister and I made our way toward the airport exit. It was my first time riding an escalator. I was entertained by how they worked. The first time around, I accidentally went up them the wrong way. My sister got a good chuckle out of that. The moment was worth it to catch a glimpse of her smile. By the third one, I got the hang of it. Just as the escalator neared the top and we could see the people and places in the main terminal, there he was. My brother. Just like my sister, I knew who he was the moment I laid eyes on him.

I ran off the escalator, dropped my luggage and everything I had in my hands, then embraced him so tight you couldn't have fit a slip of paper between us. I couldn't stop staring at him. Finally. I'd recovered the last missing piece of my childhood and we stood, face to face, right there in the middle of JFK.

My brother invited us to stay at his apartment with him and his roommate. I was glad because it would give us even more time together. Between work and other commitments, our trip was going to be a short one. We arrived on a Thursday and our all-too-soon flight home was on Sunday. We knew we only had a short time together, so we were determined to make the best of it. But how do you cram thirteen years into seventy-two hours?

We went back to his apartment and sat down all together to read the online version of the *Asheville Citizen-Times'* second article. As we read it together, our brother started filling in the missing pieces about us. Matthew learned how Melissa and I found each other, what was going on in our lives, and how we ended up where we were. My brother didn't want to talk about his past or what his foster homes had been like. I think he wanted to focus on the present and the future, not the past. Afterwards, we sat and talked until three in the morning. I barely slept that night. I had hundreds of emotions running through me, but most of all, gratitude. For the first time, we were all together under one roof—without Martha.

> For the first time, we were all together under one roof—without Martha.

The three of us spent the following day touring the city. We took the Staten Island ferry over to Lady Liberty, tasted our way through the number-one rated food spots in the city, and then topped off our day by indulging ourselves at the iconic Serendipity 3. It was the perfect day—just the three of us in this big city with no interruptions.

I still had so many questions, but knew my brother couldn't answer them. Most of all, I wanted to know about my mother. What did she look like? Did I have her smile? Does she wear glasses? Was she still in Morocco? Why did she let me go? What about my father? Does he know I'm alive? Is he alive?

I mentioned all of this to my brother when we got back to his apartment. He paused the conversation and left the room for a second. When he returned, he had a folder in his hands. "I have a letter from our aunt in Holland," he told me. He went on to explain that, at some point while he was in foster care, he'd been given some information about his origins. With that information, he had tracked her down and they had been writing to each other for a while.

The letter was faded, the edges of the pages creased and worn, her writing vintage cursive. It looked like it had traveled many miles to reach its final destination. It was eight pages long and filled with answers to questions that had haunted me all my life.

Chapter 9

DNA

There she was. My mother.

My aunt had included photos with her letter. In one of them, my brother was sitting on my mother's lap on a floral print couch surrounded by two older women. That was the first time I had ever laid eyes on my mother. I never had a memory of a hug, a kiss, or a meal cooked by her.

That was the first time I had ever laid eyes on my mother.

I couldn't get over how much we looked alike. The shape of her nose, the curve of her chin, even the glasses on her face were as similar to mine as a twin's. There was no denying that she was my mother.

As happy as I was to finally see a picture of her, it also made me sad. I looked at her image and wondered what had transpired in her life that led to her decision to grow old without her children.

Had she even had a choice, or did she let us go on purpose?

My feelings about my mother are complicated—a mixture of anger, guilt, and sorrow. It's almost impossible to have an emotional reaction to the image of "Mom" because I don't really know anything about her other than what she looks like. There are two sides to every story and I don't know either side, not really.

A while back, I did get the chance to talk to her on the phone. The call was cut short because the language barrier made it impossible for us to understand each other. People often ask me if I want to meet her someday. Absolutely. We all have our own story. Perhaps her story helped us have a better life. You can't judge people for their actions. All you can do is try to understand the why and offer them grace and compassion.

There was one, singular thing I realized that day—I was far from alone anymore. According to my aunt's letter, I had family members in Belgium, France, the Netherlands, Germany, Morocco, and Finland. My mother, who had come from a family of eight, lived in Germany with one of her younger brothers. Three hundred people dispersed throughout Europe were linked to my DNA. They were a combination of aunts, uncles, nephews and nieces, as well as first and second cousins. All of these people shared one other thing in common—they had never met me. They didn't know my name and they had no idea what I looked like.

The time spent in New York City with my brother was like holding the winning ticket to a billion-dollar jackpot. I struggled at the airport; I wasn't ready for the goodbye hugs and the distance between us. The last time we said goodbye I didn't see him again for thirteen years. He reassured us that he would keep the lines of communication open and would be in touch very soon.

Back home, I tried to process how I'd gone from not knowing a single thing about my family to knowing I had dozens of family members all over the world. It was crazy to think these people existed thousands of miles away, and there I was, living my quiet life in a small town in North Carolina. I decided to become the investigator of my own life and started by reaching out to my aunt. I wanted to discover as much as possible about my past and had a burning desire to learn all I could about this woman who was supposedly my mother.

My aunt had given my brother an email address, so I shot off an email to her and got a reply a few days later. My Aunt Nancy was married to my mother's brother, Fazal. She shared with me what few details she knew about the days we were in Spain. She told me where my mother was currently living, and updated me on other family members. Nancy not only emailed me, but she also sent handwritten cards for special occasions such as birthdays, holidays, or just because, with family updates and photos tucked inside. Every now and again, I pull out those photos and try to picture myself in those specific settings to see if I can trigger a memory, but I was just so young when I left that I literally have no memories of those years.

Meanwhile, my life was being lived at full speed. I had been home for a few weeks and was still trying to process everything that had transpired over the last few months. It was a lot. My emotional train was running on fumes. My brother called and said he wanted to move to North Carolina so he could be closer and we could be a family again. Even though our tiny brick house was at full occupancy, my sister and I decided we definitely had room for one more. A few months later, we were all living under the same roof. Life was good.

I knew my story was one of a kind, and still I was surprised when a reporter from *Glamour* magazine called me one day. Over the course of the next month, she and I exchanged several emails, pictures, and phone calls. We were so close to being done when the story got pulled. The timing was off with what was going on in the world. I was okay with that and felt honored just to be asked. Through the course of our conversations, one question resonated and I found a new mission. She once asked me, "Who are you?" I couldn't answer the question.

Who am I?

The next few years flew by. Janna and Shanna found the loves of their lives, got married, and had beautiful children. My brother decided to seek adventure on the Bering Sea and worked on an Alaskan crab boat for a few years before finding his wife and moving to Las Vegas. My sister, on the other hand followed the love of her life to Florida. It would be quite some time before I, too, moved away.

When my thirtieth birthday rolled around, I looked back at all that had happened and decided I was ready for a change. A change of pace and a change of scenery—a change that would bring me closer to the person I needed most in my life, my sister. I woke up one morning, stuffed my entire life into my 2008 Silver Toyota Camry Solara and headed towards the Sunshine State.

This was one time I didn't take a moment to look back, only ahead. While driving, I thought about the many possibilities the future had in store for me, and the path I would forge for myself. I wondered if I'd ever meet any of my extended family; and maybe, just maybe, I might try to find my father.

One of the letters my brother received was from the man who had dropped us off at Martha's all those years ago. I found out that not only was that man *not* our father, but that my real father lived in Pensacola, Florida. Well, according to my aunt, that's where he'd been in 1993. I don't know much else about him, not even his name for sure. The man put my father's name in quotation marks because even he wasn't sure if that was his legal name. I wondered what he looked like. If he would be proud of the person I'd become and the accomplishments I'd achieved.

Two years ago, I tore both of my Achilles tendons and was recovering from one of the surgeries. The recovery was a long one, which meant I had a lot of time to read and watch television. One day, I saw a teaser for a show called *Long Lost Family*. It was a new show on TLC about finding lost family members and reuniting them, but only within the United States. I knew that meant my mother was out of the question, but my father wasn't.

I currently have a group of friends, seven strong, inspiring, hilarious, professional women, and we have dubbed The Chicas. One afternoon, a few of them paid me a friendly visit. I told them about the show and they encouraged me to apply. They told me I didn't know what could happen and that I'd never get answers if I didn't put myself out there. Then they sat with me while I filled out the online application. I knew the odds were against me, but a life worth living is always worth taking a reasonable risk.

Four months later, I received a call from Los Angeles, California from the casting producer of *Long Lost Family*. We exchanged several phone calls and emails, and they finally asked if they could start with a DNA search. I knew my chances were slim, but I was all in. What did I have to lose?

I filled the small cylinder with saliva and sent it off. Thirty-six years of walking this earth not knowing who I was came down to sixty days of waiting. And a single phone call. Like everything else in my life, it wasn't what I expected.

Thirty-six years of walking this earth not knowing who I was came down to sixty days of waiting.

"We ran your DNA through all the databases and, unfortunately, no match was detected," the casting producer told me. I knew it had been a 50/50 chance, but I'm not going to lie; I was really disappointed. I thanked him for the opportunity and hung up the phone. While I might've lost the battle, trying to find my father, the entire process helped me gain a better perception of who I was.

Chapter 10
Today

*M*y story is much like one of my favorite poems, Robert Frost's "The Road Not Taken". The difference is that I didn't have a choice all those years ago about which path I wanted to take. The other people in my life chose a road filled with unanswered questions. I'd love to say that it's all wrapped up in a neat little bow, complete with a Hollywood ending, but that's not how real life works.

I'm thirty-seven now, but still know so little about who I am and how I got here. I know I was born in Spain and lived in Morocco for a short time. I grew up in North Carolina and now live in Florida. To this day, I still carry around a thick, white three-ring binder stuffed with pictures, court orders, letters from State Senators, cards, school records, and other fragments of the unraveled red tape that is my life. When I feel the urge to play

Sherlock Holmes, I grab a bottle of wine and start going through the binder, dissecting it piece by piece. The outcome is always the same—I'm still confused. I still don't have answers and I get angry because I just don't know the "why".

In this day and age, with pretty much everything being on the internet, one would think finding the information I wanted—no, what I needed—would be easy, but it's not. I grew up before everything was online and my entire identity was essentially papers stuffed in a file folder, packed away in the bowels of the social services system. Like many children who go through the system, documentation to identify who they are can be scarce. When a child is constantly moved from place to place, sometimes their proof of identity doesn't follow them. In many cases it gets left behind or lost in the shuffle. All I have to identify my origins is a three by five piece of paper called a "Certificate of Birth Abroad".

It might have been easier had I been adopted and had time to put down roots with one family. However, adoption was never an option for me. Since I didn't know who my parents were, the courts couldn't terminate their paternal rights to make room for a new family to choose me. I try not to dwell on the negatives and instead focus on the positives. Because I don't have much of a family,

I try not to dwell on the negatives and instead focus on the positives.

I get to choose who comes in and out of my life. I've been privileged and blessed with so many friendships. Each person I've met along the way has kept my soul energized and enriched my life in some way. I may not have a family linked by DNA, but what I do have is a tribe of friends who make up the story of my life. So many people have made a difference I couldn't count them any easier than I could count grains of sand on a beach.

Some of the people I met and connected with came in and out of my life quickly; they were a temporary presence. There has, however, been one constant. God. The bond I have with Him is eternal. He's never lost sight of me. When I was broke, He provided me with ways to get by. When I was sad, He was there to wipe away my tears. And when I was lost, He sent total strangers to light my path. I may not always regularly attend church, or spend a lot of time with my Bible, but I still hold on to my faith. Every time my faith gets shaky, God does something I can't explain. I never question those moments, I just believe.

Today, I have the honor of working at the leading professional services networks in the world, PwC. They have helped me live a purpose-driven life and always inspire me to bring my whole self to work. To not only do my best, but to stretch my wings a little more every day. When I'm not at work, I donate my time to help children in the foster care system. I advocate for the voiceless and help prepare those who have aged out of the system gain the proper tools and skills to navigate a successful road towards independence. I enjoy speaking and never want to pass up an opportunity to encourage others to own their story—to dream big and be proud of who they are. For me, sharing my story is cathartic.

I firmly believe that we are given one life to live and that no matter what cards we are dealt, we have a choice in how we play our hand. No one can tell you how to live your life. You make it what you want it to be, and you have the choice to see the things you go through as drawbacks or blessings. If my life was a movie and I had the choice to rewind and reshoot scenes I didn't like, I would always press play to see what will happen next. If I hadn't experienced the obstacle course of foster care, I wouldn't be the person I am today. Most of all, I've realized I am strong and can weather the strongest of hurricanes.

In the process, I've discovered so much about myself—my character and who I am as a friend, sister, aunt, and colleague. I didn't know the true meaning of being an aunt until the moment my sister gave me the best gift ever, getting to be an aunt to her daughter, Teagan. Her beautiful and gentle spirit lightens my world every day and my hope is to always make her proud and encourage her to live her life like a butterfly.

My story is not a dotted line from A to B, and for all I know the next chapter will take me to Africa, Europe, or maybe just the next town over. Recent discoveries indicate that there is another young man somewhere in the world who might be another brother of mine. How many more siblings do I have? Will fate step in again and bring him into my life? One day, I hope I get the chance to find the people who created and molded me into the human I am today, but to also finally figure out why I'm anything but ordinary!

More than 40% of the children who reach the age of 18 while in foster care were in the system for more than 3 years.

Chapter 11

To Foster Kids

As I said at the beginning of this book, foster kids are resilient. Resilience is the ability to adapt and achieve positive outcomes despite adversity. So many of the other foster kids I knew had this quality, and I know I do too.

Resilience is the ability to adapt and achieve positive outcomes despite adversity.

If you are in the foster care system, your life is often in upheaval. The future is uncertain. Some families will be great and some will be terrible. It's important that you create a foundation for yourself. You won't always have other people to do it for you, so creating one yourself gives you the building blocks you need to stand strong, no matter what life throws your way.

Over the years, I developed a personal system for approaching life. I had so many odds stacked against me, yet I was determined to not only thrive, but to succeed. Whenever I faced a challenge or a decision, I relied on these five beliefs:

Understanding: The first tenet in my system is learning to understand other people. Don't judge others right away. Try to see the world from their perspective. Other people's opinions and behavior are often due to their past experiences. By giving people understanding before judgment, you are giving them grace. I know it's hard to trust and that you want to keep your armor in place, but there are some genuinely good people in the world who truly want to help you and better your life.

Set Goals: All my life I have set goals, both long and short-term. My short-term goal was the same every day—to be the best person I could be. Albert Einstein once said, "Try not to become a man of success, but rather try to become a man of value." That's what I want—to be a person of value. Success is secondary.

However, I was just as driven to achieve my long-term goals. When I was in high school, I had no idea how I was going to afford a college education. But it was my biggest dream and I was determined to make it happen. It took a lot of hard work and dedication to make it to all my classes, maintain good grades, and still work four or five jobs to pay the bills. My education has benefited me in so many ways. I now have a great career and work with wonderful people.

Another long-term goal is to meet my parents. I want them to see the person I have become, as well as understand the why behind their decisions.

Be Responsible: You may have to grow up much faster than other kids who aren't in the foster care system. You are probably going to have to be more responsible for yourself than other kids. But that's okay—learning to be responsible prepares you for adulthood. Be courageous and be a leader. In doing so, you might discover the same thing I did when I stepped out of my own shadow—skills and talents you didn't even know you had. Apply to every job you can. Be prepared for every interview you go on with the understanding you may not get the job. Don't take a no as you're not good enough, use it as an experience. Don't be afraid to take chances.

A Belief System: We all see the world through our own individual lenses. Whether your belief system is built on God or not is up to you, but having some structure for what is right and wrong will serve you well when you need to make tough decisions. With faith and love in your life, you can accomplish anything.

Know Your Value: You are a valuable person. You are not a throwaway or a case file. There is value in the gifts you bring to the world, gifts you were given for a reason. Don't let other people put you down or convince you that you don't have value. You do, and you have since your very first breath. Know your value, believe in it, and hold on to it every single day. Go live the life you deserve.

Every experience I have gone through has taught me something about myself. Those moments, while hard, gave me the knowledge that I am strong, far stronger than I ever realized or believed. You are, too.

So set your goals, know your worth, and hold on to the people who care about you. Those people can be your foundation when your life is shaky. They can be role models when you aren't sure how to act. They can be the family you choose when you miss the family you lost.

I hope my story has inspired you. If it has, feel free to email me and let me know. To me, you're not a foster child— you're another friend I have yet to meet.

Chapter 12
Foster Parent Tips

*I*f you are a foster parent, this chapter is for you. First, thank you for taking in a child who has nowhere else to go. I know there will be challenging days, because these are children who have been battered and bruised by life. They are slow to trust, reluctant to open up, and expect to be let down. You can change their lives, even if you are only a part of it for a short while. Foster parents are extraordinary individuals who are on this earth to give children a second chance at life.

As a society, we have an important part to play in the lives of the children put through the foster care system. When they live with you, there is a short window of opportunity for you to make a difference that will positively affect their adult life. These children are not looking for perfect people, but rather people who are willing to see them just as they are and be willing to say *yes, I want to help*

> These children are not looking for perfect people, but rather people who are willing to see them just as they are and be willing to say *yes, I want to help you.*

you. Foster children are not statistics, they are children who have a full future ahead of them. Love them and support them as you would your own child.

Even at thirty-seven, there is still a huge void in my heart because I lacked parents of any form. All a foster kid wants is a connection with you. Below are a few tips for being a great foster parent, written from the perspective of a former foster child.

1. **Maintain Routines.** We all need a sense of security in our lives. When a child has been removed from his or her home, even if that home was a nightmare, they are leaving behind everything they have ever known. Losing that, even if it's the best thing for them, also means they lose security. It's important for foster parents to build that foundation right away. So create a routine for breakfast, getting to school, doing homework, going to bed. Routines create security—they give kids stability and instill a sense of predictability in them. Most foster kids have lived in chaos from birth, so routines help them find solid footing, which leads to trust and connection.

2. **Build A Relationship.** Don't get discouraged if the child in your home is distant, or even cold to you. These children come from all walks of life and have been put into uncomfortable circumstances. They are reluctant to trust—adults have let them down over and over again, and their lives have been in upheaval for years. Have patience and spend time in those first few weeks to get to know them on a personal and deeper level. Don't push that relationship, just stay there with them in the moment and constantly let them know you are there for them. Listen to what they say they want and need, and then try to discover the wants and needs they keep to themselves. Smile often and share hugs. Treat them as one of your own children and realize that it will take time to create a bond. Trust and relationships don't happen overnight. It may take months or perhaps years before you gain their trust. Work to build a relationship one moment at a time, and trust will soon follow.

3. **Have Fun.** It is often said that laughter is good for the soul. I believe it. After the trauma these children have faced, laughter might very well be the best medicine for them. Carve out time in their routine to

have some fun as a family. Go bowling, canoeing, and jump on trampolines. Play silly games at the dinner table or simply watch a comedy together. If the child doesn't join in right away, that's okay—go back to numbers one and two. Be open and loving, and never give up. When a child is having fun, they are more accepting, active, and enjoying life with YOU!

4. **Don't Label.** I've never been a big fan of the word "foster" before the words child and parent. But it's a stamp placed there by society. One of the biggest ways to make a child feel like they don't belong with you is to put a label before their name. Be careful how you introduce your child. NEVER put their family status before their name. Always introduce the child as "Liz, my foster child" instead of "my foster child, Liz". Make him or her feel like an individual, someone you are proud to have as part of your family. Please don't label them. Labels belong on cans, not children.

5. **Accept Them into the Family.** We all want that one thing: to be accepted. When a child has just had their world turned upside down, the most important step to take is making that child feel like they belong. Help them see their value and what they

can contribute to your life as a parent. Never exclude the child from family activities and make every effort to introduce them to your whole family. Help them find a place they can call home.

You can never go wrong with love. Love these kids, give them breathing room and support them as they try to find their footing. They are there with you for reasons to great for you to comprehend.

I truly believe that our lives are already planned before we are born. We are directed down certain paths and introduced to certain people. There is a strategic reason for why we are placed in each other's lives. Foster children and foster parents are all there for a certain reason. Try to make it the best experience possible for everyone.

If you're not seeking to become a foster parent, there are still ways you can get involved:

1. Support aged-out youth once they leave foster care

2. Be a mentor to a foster child

3. Be a Guardian Ad Litem

4. Donate clothes, bikes, school supplies, etc. to foster child organizations

5. Donate laptops, tablets, or Kindles to children in need

6. Provide transportation to and from appointments

7. Make blankets to share with foster kids

8. Educate yourself about the foster care system and become an advocate

9. Support a local cause that supports foster care and adoption

10. Make a holiday meal for a group home

Resources and References

If you'd like more information, check out these sources:

National Foster Care and Adoption Directory Search: https://childwelfare.gov/nfcad/

National Court Appointed Special Advocates (CASA): http://www.casaforchildren.org

National Foster Care Coalition: http://www.nationalfostercare.org/

AdoptUsKids: https://www.adoptuskids.org/

Heart Gallery of America, Inc.: https://www.heartgalleryofamerica.org/Kids/

FosterClub: https://www.fosterclub.com/

Eckerd Connects: https://eckerd.org/

Foster Care to Success: http://www.fc2success.org/

Children's Rights: http://www.childrensrights.org/

National Foster Youth Institute:
https://www.nfyi.org/

American Society for the Positive Care of
Children: https://americanspcc.org/

In the Tampa Bay area:

Eckerd Connects: www.eckerd.org

Eckerd Connects Raising Hope:
www.eckerd.org/raisinghope

Camelot Community Care:
http://www.camelotcommunitycare.org/

Friends of Joshua House Foundation:
www.friendsofjoshuahouse.org

The Children's Home Network:
www.childrenshomenetwork.org

The Florida Statewide Guardian ad Litem (GAL)
Program: www.GuardianadLitem.org

Grow Into You Foundation:
www.growintoyoufoundation.org

Ready For Life:
http://www.readyforlifepinellas.org/

In the Waynesville, North Carolina area:

Baptist Children's Home of North Carolina: www.bchfamily.org/help/foster_care

Youth Villages: www.youthvillages.org/

Children's Hope Alliance: www.childrenshopealliance.org/

Foster Grandparent Program: www.mountainprojects.org/foster-grandparent-program

Family and Children Services: www.haywoodnc.net

Black Mountain Home for Children, Youth and Families: www.blackmountainhome.org

Eliada Group Home: www.eliada.org

Foster Care Terminology

Adoption: The process people go through to become a child's legal parent.

Foster Family Agency: A private agency that certifies and supervises foster homes.

Aging Out: Youth who exit the foster care system at the age of eighteen.

Child Advocate: A person who gets to know the child and advocates for the best interest and the wishes of the child.

Department of Family and Children's Services (DFCS): A department within each county that works ensure the safety and protection of children. Whenever possible, it helps them to remain in their own homes or return home as soon as possible.

Dependent Child: A child who is a dependent of the court.

Family Reunification (FR): Court-ordered services offered by DFCS in an attempt to return children to their birth parents.

Foster Care: The formal care and protection of non-relative children.

Independent Living Program (ILP): ILP is a DFCS program that works with foster care youth age sixteen to twenty-one years old with issues such as education, employment, living skills, and much more.

Juvenile Court: Deals with dependent children.

Permanent Placement: An adoptive home, guardian home, or long-term foster home that will take care of the child permanently.

Relative: According to each state's Welfare and Institution code, a "relative" refers to any adult related to the child by blood, adoption, or affinity within the fifth degree of kinship. This includes stepparents, step siblings, and all relatives whose status is preceded by the words: "great", "great-great", or "grand", or the spouse of any of these persons, even if the marriage was terminated by death or dissolution.

Sibling Contact: Visitation between children in the same family. Often times sibling contact is ordered by the court or set up by the social worker(s).

Social Worker: Any of various professional activities or methods concretely concerned with providing social services and especially with the investigation, treatment, and material aid of the economically, physically, mentally, or socially disadvantaged.

Temporary Custody: When a child is reported to be in danger, a social worker or police officer will respond to the child's location to assess the safety of the child(ren). If the child is assessed to be in an immediate unsafe situation, the child will be taken into temporary "protective custody", usually by the police officer and transported to the Children's Shelter Care System.

Unsupervised Visit: Visitation between a child and his or her birth parent or relative without the supervision of a third party.

Reference: https://helponechild.org/families/ foster-care-resources/glossary-of-terms

An Open Letter to Walmart

Dear Walmart,

I want to say thank you for the five wonderful years I spent at the Murphy, North Carolina store. I'm very proud to have been a Walmart associate, and will never forget how that job changed my life.

In August 1998, I was an ordinary young woman walking inside the store for my first day as an employee. At the time, I felt lost and misplaced. I didn't know where I belonged in that small town, let alone the world. I had no family. Heck, I didn't even know the true meaning of family. I always thought the only way you were family was to be connected by DNA. I was afraid of what people would think if they found out that I was an orphan and grew up in foster care.

I didn't know exactly what to expect when I started working at store #0515. In those early days, I treated it as any other job, a means to make a living. Show up, work my shift and head home. I had lived my life that way for so long, a tape that was always on repeat. As the months passed and I started to get to know the store managers and other associates on the floor, something began to change. My eagerness to head home after my shift faded. I was happy to come to work and excited to welcome every customer with, "How May I Help You?" I enjoyed the dynamics of the store, the variety of customers, the warm and welcoming associates, and all the different departments where I worked. When I was in college and needed a place to go for the holidays, Walmart allowed me the ability to work my own schedule so that I wouldn't be alone. Before I knew it, years had flown by. I was commuting two hours just to work sixteen, and looking forward to every shift. I woke up one day and realized Walmart had become home to me.

Walmart, you blessed me with so many opportunities that went beyond the cash register. You provided me with a set of skills that made sure I could succeed at anything I attempted. You gave me connections that will last a lifetime, a group of associates who took the time to get to know me as a person, not just another employee. Not once did I feel like I couldn't come to work as my whole self. I always felt supported, valued and loved. You saw the potential that I had inside me, nurtured my skills and talents, and gave me the opportunity to excel.

In January 2003, I walked through your doors for the last time as an employee. I didn't leave with just my Walmart badge and blue smock in hand, I left with more than I could have ever imagined. A family and the knowledge that I could make a difference in the world. Walmart, you were a home when I needed one, and you always will be.

Thank you for helping me rewrite my story.

Liz

Chapter 5 – My favorite name badge

About the Author

Liz Sutherland grew up with no identity. She has no memory of the first few years of her life, outside of being dropped off at a stranger's house when she was a child. Liz and her siblings lived in an abusive home with a woman they were told was their grandmother, until  Liz gathered the courage to call social services and rescue herself and her siblings. Thrust into the foster care system, she learned to survive but never gave up hope that she might someday be reunited with her brother and sister and discover the truth about her identity.

Demonstrating remarkable resilience, she graduated from Western Carolina University with degrees in Computer Information Systems & Criminal Justice. She now works in Tampa and has her own blog, talking about her search for her family. She was featured in the book Growing Up In The Care of Strangers and is the author of *No Ordinary Liz*, a book chronicling her incredible life story. She is a frequent speaker for organizations such as the Women of Compassion Forum, 4Kids, and the Junior League of Tampa Bay.

To Connect with Liz:

Email: Noordinaryliz@hotmail.com

Facebook: www.facebook.com/noordinaryliz

Twitter: www.twitter.com/noordinaryliz

Instagram: www.instagram.com/noordinaryliz

Blog: www.noordinaryliz.com

LinkedIn: linkedin/in/ElizabethSutherland

Chapter 1 – Feeling displaced and abandoned

Chapter 1 – Me in my favorite church dress

Chapter 1 – Entrance to trailer park

Chapter 1 – My sister, brother and I

Chapter 5 – The perfect strangers, Evelyn & Gene

Chapter 6 – The sweet family of Rhondi, Jif, Janna & Shanna

Chapter 7 – My proudest accomplishment

Chapter 7 – My sister and I today